PIP AND BUNNY: PIP'S DREAM

The invaluable 'Pip and Bunny' collection is a set of six picture books with an accompanying handbook and e-resources carefully written and illustrated to support the development of visual and literary skills. By inspiring conversation and imagination, the books promote emotional and social literacy in the young reader.

Designed for use within the early years setting or at home, each story explores different areas of social and emotional development. The full set includes:

- six beautifully illustrated picture books with text and vocabulary for each
- a handbook designed to guide the adult in using the books effectively
- 'Talking Points' relating to the child's own world
- 'What's the Word?' picture pages to be photocopied, downloaded or printed for language development
- detailed suggestions as to how to link with other EYFS areas of learning.

The set is designed to be used in both individual and group settings. It will be a valuable resource for teachers, SENCOs (preschool and reception), Early Years Staff (nursery, preschool and reception), EOTAs, Educational Psychologists, Counsellors and Speech Therapists.

Maureen Glynn has 25 years' experience teaching primary and secondary age children in mainstream, home school and special school settings, in the UK and Ireland.

First published 2020
by Routledge
2 Park Square, Milton Park, Abingdon, Oxon OX14 4RN

and by Routledge
52 Vanderbilt Avenue, New York, NY 10017

Routledge is an imprint of the Taylor & Francis Group, an informa business

British Library Cataloguing-in-Publication Data
A catalogue record for this book is available from the British Library

Library of Congress Cataloging-in-Publication Data
A catalog record for this book has been requested

ISBN: 978-0-367-18839-9 (pbk)
ISBN: 978-0-429-35493-9 (ebk)

Typeset in Calibri
by Apex CoVantage, LLC

Visit www.Routledge.com/9780367136642

Book 1 Pip's Dream

Pip loves Bunny.

This story tells what happened one night
whilst Pip dreamt and the moon shone bright.

Pip and Bunny are asleep.
Suddenly there's a noise
outside.

Pip wakes up.

She tosses and turns.

Turns and tosses.
Tosses and turns.
Oh no!

'Where's Bunny?' Pip cries.

Is she ...

Under the duvet?

Under the pillow?

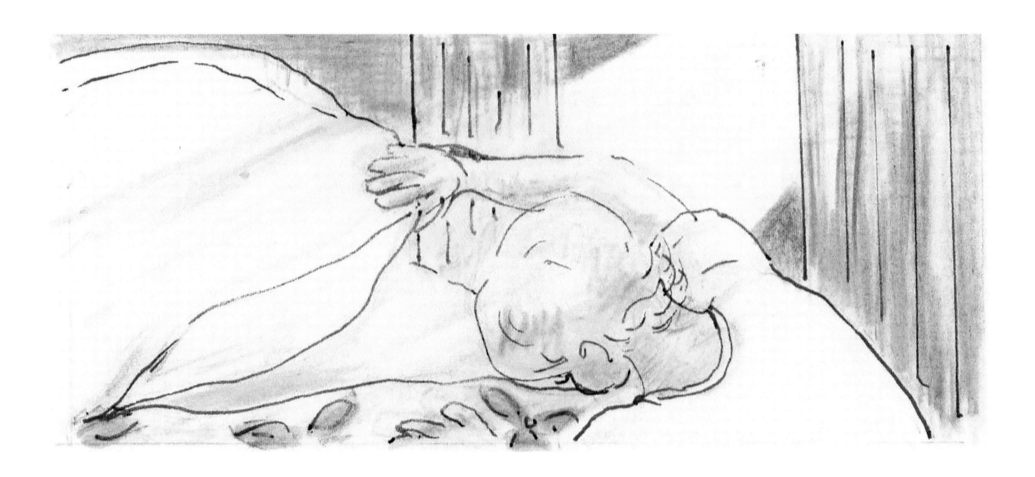

Under the bed?

'Ooh-ooh!
Where can she be?'

Pip creeps out of bed.

She looks in her wigwam.

But Bunny's not there.
Pip looks around her
bedroom.

'There you are!'
Pip finds Bunny lying in the moonlight.

Sweet dreams Pip and Bunny!

As Pip sleeps, she dreams of a walk in the park with Bunny.

They come to a stile.

Where does that go to? Pip wonders.

They walk on...
Someone's watching!

'Listen Bunny.'
'Look up there!'

Deeper into the wood they go.

Suddenly,
in the clearing they
find...

not one, not two, not three,
but seven bunnies all having
fun!

Pip and Bunny enjoy a great time there.

Then they wake up.

Book 1 Pip's Dream What's the Word?

Show the page and ask the child to say words that explain each image:

Page 22 Action Words?

Page 23 Location Words?

Page 24 Sound Words?

Page 25 Light Words?

Page 26 Emotions and Feelings?

Action Words?

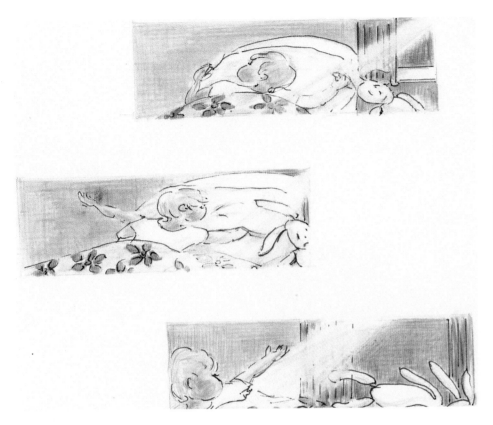

Location Words?

Sound Words?

Light Words?

25

Emotions and Feelings?